# MITCH MURRAY'S

## COMPLETE BOOK OF

# ONE-LINERS

### FOR

# WEDDINGS

•

## And how to use them in your speech

# MITCH MURRAY'S

## COMPLETE BOOK OF

# *ONE-LINERS*

## FOR

# *WEDDINGS*

•

## *And how to use them in your speech*

foulsham

LONDON • NEW YORK • TORONTO • SYDNEY

# foulsham

Bennetts Close, Cippenham, Berks, SL1 5AP

Edited by Carole Chapman

ISBN 0-572-01896-7

Copyright © 1995 Mitch Murray

Typeset in Great Britain by Typesetting Solutions, Slough, Berks
Printed in Great Britain by St Edmundsbury Press Ltd, Bury St Edmunds, Suffolk

# At last! At last!

I've been **dying** to place on record, my gratitude to the most generous and supportive friend a man could wish to have.

For many years, I've been very fortunate to have Bob Monkhouse as my special mentor. At last I am able to make a small gesture of appreciation for all his help and encouragement.

I'm therefore delighted to have the opportunity of dedicating this work, the first in my series, to Bob Monkhouse O.B.E.

It was almost worth writing the book for that reason alone.

# Contents

# Introduction

You can't fool me! I know exactly why you've bought this book; you have a speech to make and you mustn't let them down.

You've seen others try:

- an embarrassingly drunk best man trying to tell risqué stories that nobody wants to hear . . .
- the groom who doesn't want to spoil his macho image by speaking affectionately about his bride . . .
- the father of the bride, desperately trying to hide the fact that he can't stand that swine of a new son-in-law!

You've seen their speeches fail, you've seen the guests squirm and now it's **your** turn.

You've been lumbered haven't you? That's why you've bought this book. Admit it.

We authors are very clever. We **know** these things.

For instance, I happen to know you only have three requirements for this speech:

1 You want it to be witty.
2 You want it to be effective.
3 You want it to be **over!**

The good news is, that's exactly what your audience want as well. I'm here to help.

Of course, as this may well be the only speech you're likely to be asked to make for several years, you won't want to start wading through a text book packed with intricate training techniques in the art of presentation and creativity; who's got time to read all that crap? ... I haven't even got time to **write** it.
So instead, how about this?

I'll show you how to prepare your own speech and I'll supply you with a rich selection of ideas, one-liners and quotations you may wish to include.

I'll let you in on some of my sneakier tricks of the trade; techniques designed to overcome the pitfalls of standing up and speaking in public.

I'll offer you advice on style and delivery and we'll look at the options of whether you should learn your speech or read it.

Taken together, these ideas will go a long way towards tackling the paradox which faces most public speakers at one time or another and which, suddenly, is now facing you. Namely, how can you hope to instil confidence in your audience when you yourself are in imminent danger of a serious laundry problem?!

At this point, you're probably tempted to skip a few pages and go straight to the section appropriate to the particular speech you have to make. I know you're anxious, but there are some important notes for you to read about first, so please stay with it for now. (Of course, if you went forward earlier and found yourself redirected to this page ... Hi there. Welcome back!)

# The Programme

At most weddings, the conventional programme begins with the **bride's father**, who proposes a toast to the bride and groom.

The **groom** replies and, in turn, proposes a toast to the bridesmaids.

At this point, tradition seems to reflect sexist and ageist values by assuming that the bridesmaids are either helplessly giggly and incompetent, or too young to stand up and speak without dribbling. To the rescue comes the **best man** who replies on their behalf and often proves to be ... yes ... giggly, incompetent **and** a dribbler!

Each one of these three speeches has its own individual character:

Our opener:

## THE FATHER OF THE BRIDE

The father of the bride is usually the straight man of the wedding speech set. Guests at the wedding party can be counted upon to treat his contribution with genial respect; after all, let's be fair, this sucker's picking up the tab.

Daddy is expected to say a few reasonably sober, sensitive yet witty words. He also has to include some love

and affection. Now that takes **sincerity**, and if you can fake sincerity, you've got it made!
(Don't worry; I have a 'Sincerity Section' later in the book.)

Second on the bill . . .

## THE BRIDEGROOM

As if he didn't have enough to worry about on his wedding day, the bridegroom's speech is expected to be middle-of-the-road; not too schmaltzy but not too biting. He needs to be amusing, but he'd better be careful; should he upset his lovely new bride on her big day, he'll soon learn that beauty and the beast are the same person!

Finally, the star of the show . . .

## THE BEST MAN

This guy thinks he's a wit . . . and he's probably half right! He's expected to roast the bridegroom and to show no mercy. If he can do this without embarrassing the poor turkey in front of the opposition, he's a hero!

☆  ☆  ☆

We'll be looking at these speeches in some detail a little farther on, but first, let's examine some important common factors.

# THE TRIBUTE

Any social speech should be looked upon as a tribute. The best man, for instance, even though his offering may be littered with insults, is still paying his friend a great compliment. He has taken the trouble of preparing a few special words and has gathered up the necessary courage to deliver his speech. This, surely, must rank as one of the most flattering wedding presents.

But **any** speech – social, political or corporate – can only ever be an exercise in superficiality. Think about it; you have only a very short time to get your points across, during which, hopefully, your audience will be glued to their seats. Come to think of it, with the right glue, it could work!

Your speech needs catchy words and humour, **but no real depth.** You have only about seven minutes and you simply can't go into detail. Social speech-making is not a medium which allows you the luxury of expanding and embellishing your thoughts. Give a speech too much substance and it becomes a lecture. People, nowadays, are programmed to absorb **soundbites.** These spoken headlines have to be linked together with little verbal bridges and need to follow a logical path. You'll see what I'm getting at later in the book, once you've looked at some examples. With this technique, however, one word in the wrong place and you've blown the joke. So a little farther on, I'll be showing you how to minimise that risk.

If I'm in the mood.

# Putting it Together

Before you start trawling the ocean of one-liners, it's important that you take a little time to learn what to do with your catch once it's landed.

## RHYTHM AND STYLE

A good speech, like a good song, needs a regular beat. It should have a rhythm of its own; peaks, troughs, crescendos and a climax. (Don't you love it when I talk dirty?)
Now, I can't start teaching you all that stuff in this little book, can I? Or **can** I?
By George, I think I can!

You see, if your material is structured properly, the rhythm of that speech, along with its highs and lows, happens almost automatically.

So let's not think too deeply about it; I'm going to recommend that your speech is a cleverly crafted succession of strong one-liners in a natural, flowing format.

That's it. No long jokes, no anecdotes, no stories . . . **one-liners.** (I should point out that I'm using the term 'one-liners' in a very generalised way; sometimes you'll be using two or three-line gags, sometimes the one-liner won't be a funny line at all – it could be a sentimental comment or piece of prose.)

In my opinion, the one-liner construction is ideal for wedding speeches; the rhythm is simple to maintain, your investment shows a return every seven or eight seconds and the format creates the illusion of a shorter, snappier speech – very handy if you're not exactly an experienced orator. If a joke or a comment falls flat . . . so what? You're straight into the next line and, chances are, nobody will even notice that your one-liner didn't work.

On the other hand, the longer story or anecdote is an investment which **has** to pay off. If a thirty second story dies a death, you have a real problem!
We've all suffered the bloke who genuinely thinks he's a raconteur but in reality couldn't tell the difference between a comma and a coma!

There are occasions, however, when an incident or an amusing episode is so well known that you will be expected to make some mention of it. Don't repeat the whole story (unless you're a Peter Ustinov). As an experience, it may have been funny if you were there at the time, but as part of an otherwise fast-moving speech, you risk losing your audience. The trick is merely to **allude** to the event by using an appropriate one-liner.

For instance, let's assume many of the guests are aware that the bridegroom decided to cook for his fiancée one night and, as a result, both of them came down with food poisoning . . .

just include the little-known fact that Dave attended the
**Karate School of Cookery** . . .
he was trained to kill with just one chop.
The bride's recent mishap with her new automobile could
be acknowledged by saying; "I wish people would stop
going on about how she handles a car . . . for God's sake, if
you don't like the way she drives, get off the pavement!!"
The sad story of a chip pan fire could be covered by a
mock telegram from Red Adair . . .

Get the picture?

There's another very good reason to avoid anecdotes and
reminiscences in wedding speeches; at a typical reception,
half the guests probably won't know the other half. Do
you really think that the bride's Auntie Phoebe genuinely
gives a toss about how the best man and the bridegroom
collaborated with the Manneken Pis to raise the water
level of that fountain in Brussels during a football
weekend? Can you honestly imagine the groom's work
mates being enthralled at stories involving an eight year
old girl's pink bootees and a cat?

The speech has to be entertaining, even to people who've
never met the characters you're talking about. Your
speech has to stand up by itself . . . and by the way, so do
you . . . so don't get too canned until it's all over.

While you're waiting to speak, level with yourself . . . are
you slurring words? are you liable to sway? . . . or see double? . . . or burp? . . . or worse? If the answer to any of these
questions is "yeshh", don't be too alarmed; at least you've
proved that the alcohol is working properly. However, as
a speech-maker, you have a problem. You must switch
immediately to water. I know, I know . . . it's **horrible**
stuff, and yes, I **do** realise what fishes do in it, but you've

swallowed too much poison and water is the antidote.

Trust me; my brother-in-law's a **dentist!** (Mind you, that's all water under the bridge.)

Drink as much water as you can as fast as you can, whether you feel like it or not. Inevitably you'll suddenly find yourself doing a lot of travelling, but that's just nature's way of helping the water to circulate around your system. You should be straightened out within ten to fifteen minutes, but keep that water handy; you'll need it **during** your speech . . . and here's why:

Nerves have a really interesting effect upon an inexperienced speaker. Your mouth suddenly dries up. It feels like someone has stuffed a ball of blotting paper into it. As you try to speak, your tongue sticks to the roof of your mouth and you suddenly wish you had teflon gums!

It's a most peculiar phenomenon and one which requires a good supply of water most of the way through your speech.

But let's turn this into an advantage . . .

Use the glass of water as a prop. It can have the same effect as George Burns's cigar; a punctuation device assisting in the control of your audience.

After you hit 'em with a one-liner, take a drink while they're laughing – don't worry, most of the material in this book is strong enough to give you enough time to have a gargle! – after a while, you'll find the crowd will begin to co-operate with you by stretching out their laughs until you've finished drinking.

People really are **dumb** aren't they?

**NOTE:** Don't forget, once your speech is over, go straight back to alcohol ... after all, you don't want to make a habit of this **water** thing, do you? Just think ... if water can rot the soles of your shoes, imagine what it can do to your stomach!

Making a speech for the first time is very much like making love for the first time. Because you may not have total confidence in what you're doing, the temptation is to rush it. She's going to change her mind ... I'm going to lose it ... we're going to be interrupted ... oh.

You don't really know for sure whether your speech is going to be well received or not ... Is the material funny enough? Is that one-liner in poor taste? Am I trying too hard?

Your audience will be slower to react at the beginning of your piece than at the end. Although you may know each one of them really well as individuals, together they have become an audience and you have become a speaker. As such you're new to each other. You need to reassess your relationship. You need to learn about them as an audience and they need to get the hang of you as a speaker. That's why they're liable to be slower at the beginning of your speech than they will be at the end.

Rushing into the next line too early is a sign that you are losing your nerve. Control it. As you deliver a line, wait just a little before you jump in with the next. Sometimes a gag will produce a delayed reaction and by the time the laughter builds up to its peak, you're halfway through the next line if you're not careful. So let the laughter run its course, and when it's just beginning to taper off, come in strong with the next gag.

You have to be sensible about this of course. Don't stand up there in total silence; if a joke dies, bury it with the next.

By the time you're about halfway through the speech, you'll find that you are actually **conducting** the audience as you would an orchestra.
Don't feel guilty; they **love** being controlled. In show-business, there's a technical name for people who really know how to manipulate their audiences . . . Stars.

☆     ☆     ☆

As you glance through the one-liners in this book, you may find that many of them need to be read aloud in order for you to see the joke. This illustrates how important it is to remember that you are writing for the **ear**, not for the **eye**.

Your audience will be **listening**, not **reading**. Your wording must sound natural; don't say "she is" when you'd normally say "she's" . . . don't say "I am" when you'd normally say "I'm" . . . don't say "you will", say "you'll" - unless, of course, you're deliberately **emphasising** the word "will" as in "You **will** tell your friends about this book, won't you?" Use normal language, not pseudo 'speech-talk'.

As my mother once advised her friend Celia, who was about to make an important speech; "Don't try to be clever - just be yourself."

# EDITING, PADDING AND LINKING

The one-liner format makes it easy to edit on-site. Suppose someone you intended to welcome hasn't turned up; simply skip that part of the speech and carry on with the next segment. If, despite your personality and witty presentation, you begin to sense that the audience has had enough, it's an easy matter to cut from where you are to a later section, or even straight to the close of the speech.

With our one-liner construction, the omissions shouldn't affect the flow. Most of the lines are self-contained; if you're doing two or three one-liners about the bridegroom's attempts at keeping fit, just use the best one. Make sure, however, that your link words are suitable and are not too repetitive.

So now you're thinking; "What the hell are **'link words'**?" Right? Yes, I **knew** what you were thinking . . . I told you we authors are very clever, didn't I?

'Link words' are what I call the little spoken punctuations and phrases used to move from one line or topic to another; words like "Now . . .", "Nevertheless . . .", "You know . . .", "Mind you . . .", "After all . . .".

Simply reciting pages of one-liners without the use of link words wouldn't work in a speech. You **need** them in order to bond your lines together, thereby creating the illusion of a natural progression.

Don't forget, you're coming out of a laugh into the next gag and it's more impressive for the audience to feel their laughter has forced you to pause than for you to appear as if you're throwing lines at them and hoping for the best.

You also need to 'bridge' from one subject to another in order to maintain a logical flow.

In the following example, I'm going to make three points about my victim:

1 He's lazy.
2 He's overweight.
3 He's a big drinker.

In other words, a perfectly normal average bloke.

I'll use **link words** to bond the jokes and **bridging lines** to progress through the subjects. The link words are in italics. The bridging lines are clearly indicated.

Here we go . . .

**Some people say Dave's lazy . . .**
**this is most unfair;**
**I know he had his window box paved over,**
**but what does <u>that</u> prove?**
**I prefer to call him a relaxoholic.**
*Of course,* **he's heard that hard work never**
**killed anyone . . .**
**but he's taking no chances on being its first**
**victim!**

*In fact,* he's stopped drinking coffee in the morning; it keeps him awake for the rest of the day!

*Mind you,* he's not lazy when it comes to trying to keep himself fit . . .

(Bridging Line)

He does a lot of jogging . . .
and you really have to take your hat off to him;
it's not easy to jog when you're eating a pizza!
*Nevertheless,* as you can see, he's in shape . . .
I mean, let's be fair; 'round' is a shape isn't it?
*Oh yes,* Dave watches his weight . . .
well, he can't really miss it;
it's right out there in front of him!

*You know,* at home, he even has his own parallel bars . . . one for brandy and one for scotch!

(Bridging Line)

O.K. . . . so Dave Newberry enjoys a drink . . .
what's wrong with that?
Most of the time he doesn't drink <u>anything</u>
stronger than pop.
*Mind you,* Pop will drink anything!
*To be fair,* he's cut down quite a bit;
this guy used to drink so much gin, <u>Gordon's</u>
thought he was a wholesaler! . . . etc. . . .

The above example illustrates how to use **link words**, not only for the purpose of joining lines together in a natural way, but also to keep your audience alert.

At times, it sounds as if you are **defending** the victim. However, this 'defence' is merely a device which gives you the excuse to continue laying into him.
Don't worry . . . he'll love it!
I think.

---

**NOTE:** In the various one-liners listed in this book, those suitable for bridging from one subject to the next will be specially indicated.

---

Don't be tempted to embellish a good line. If it ain't broke, don't fix it! One-liners usually contain a 'set up' and a 'sting':

> Set up:     **I'd love to see her in something long and flowing . . .**
>
> Sting:      **. . . like a <u>river</u>!**

The words "long and flowing" are crucial. They conjure up the image of a beautiful ball-gown. The audience has been 'set up' for the surprise of the 'sting' line. Change these words and you lose the point. Put a line or even an extra word between "flowing" and "river" and you weaken the impact. Your audience has to retain the memory of the 'set up' in order to realise they've been had.

Equally, if you feel you need to trim a one-liner, make sure that your cut doesn't damage the flow. Sometimes a gag can sound 'one-legged' if the rhythm is disturbed.

Think very carefully before messing about with one-liners. Be aware that certain words, which may appear innocuous or superfluous, could be part of the magic that makes us laugh. Removing those words may be fatal to the line.

Some words are simply **funny** words. For example:

| "Hen" | – | nothing | "Chicken" | – | funny |
|-------|---|---------|-----------|---|-------|
| "Gloves" | – | nothing | "Socks" | – | funny |
| "Beige" | – | nothing | "Puce" | – | funny. |

The expression: "Father-in-law" is not in the least funny, whereas "Mother-in-law" is absolutely **sidesplitting** ... at least, it would be if it wasn't so tragic!

I should point out at this juncture that I've always tried to avoid analysing comedy; it's a bit like love – if you have to define it, you don't deserve it. A line is either humorous, or it isn't. However, sometimes an illustration or two may help someone avoid ruining an otherwise funny line, so I apologise – it's a dirty job, but somebody's got to do it!

# NOTES, MEMORY OR SCRIPT

Many experts advise against writing your speech out in full. They feel that this method would make your performance sound false and contrived. I happen to differ. It ain't necessarily so. Let's look at the alternatives:

## Cue cards

To start with, I think these things are distracting and look very silly. They give the impression that you've hastily jotted down a few words on some old place-cards you found a few minutes ago in the cloak-room.

A five-minute speech could contain about fifty cues. At the normal delivery speed, your card-shuffling will very rapidly begin to fascinate the audience more than whatever you're saying.

## *Notes on a sheet of paper*

Not too bad a method for some speeches or presentations, but remember – the one-liner format in particular, requires precise construction. All sorts of things can go wrong if your notes don't trigger the correct wording.

Consider this . . .

> **We're here to celebrate a love match, pure and simple; Lucy's pure and David's . . . a very nice guy!**

Good line. Guaranteed to get a laugh. But what if your notes said "LOVE MATCH" and you delivered it like this . . .

> **We're here to celebrate a love match, plain and simple; Lucy's plain and . . . Oh shit!**

To be safe, your notes *should* have read; "CELEBRATE – LOVE MATCH – PURE & SIMPLE".

Hardly worth the bother is it? You might as well write it out in full.

## *Learn it by heart?*

Unless you have a photographic memory, a wealth of experience and nerves of steel, forget it! Because chances are, you **will**! You're going to be nervous in any case; even the most seasoned professional expects a few butterflies before he stands up. Why inflict upon yourself the added terror of forgetting your words? Believe me, when you stand up to speak, you're going to need as much confidence as you can falsify.

Instead of trying to memorise a fast-moving speech of this kind, you'd do better to utilise some of my sneakier techniques. These little tricks were designed to make the audience almost unaware that you're reading the whole thing. What's more, they work. So instead of sitting up night after night, attempting to learn fourteen hundred crucial words, use just a fraction of that time and effort to develop the knack of presenting your speech in a natural and relaxed manner.

Here's what I recommend:

Write the speech out in **full** on reasonably heavy paper, about 7 inches by 9 (17 x 24 cm). The paper shouldn't be too flimsy; the pages need to be easy to separate as you're reading.

Use felt-tip pens in varying colours; for instance, one joke or small paragraph in blue, the next in black. The following line could be in green, followed by purple, and so on.

Finally, underline certain key words in red. These could be words you need to emphasise, or merely the 'bones' of a line which could be glanced at and used as shorthand.

I'm sure you've seen speech-makers happily reading from typewritten or handwritten sheets of A4. Realising, quite rightly, that they need to look away from the script and make some eye contact with their audience from time to time, they look up and finish a line or two from memory as they glance around the room.
Then they look down again . . .
Silence . . . **more** silence . . . <u>**excruciating**</u> silence.

A desperate and embarrassing search has begun. The poor sap has lost his place!

"Where was I? Up the top? No, I've done that bit. Some-where about three quarters of the way down, I think . . . er
. . ."

Trouble is, all the words on the page look exactly the same. It's just one sheet of writing.
However, with my recommended system of using coloured text, it's much less likely that you'll lose your place.
Don't be concerned, you don't need to memorise the colour you were on before you looked away from your script; for some reason your subconscious takes care of all that. It usually leads you back to the correct place.

Practice it . . . even if it doesn't work for you one hundred percent, at least you'll be able to scan the page at a faster rate. Remember, you only have to look at the beginning of each topic to know whether it's the right one or not, and you ought only to have about eight to ten one-liners per page.

As I said at the beginning of the chapter on editing, the one-liner construction makes it much easier to cut whole sections of your speech in 'real-time' if necessary. The colourtext system makes it easier still.

## *A very sneaky ploy*

Here's a little trick to make people unaware that, in fact, you're reading your speech word for word . . .

Start off with a couple of announcements – it's perfectly natural for you to be reading these – then you can go straight into your speech, still reading . . . and they won't even notice.

This trick is ideal for the best man who, in any case, will be expected to read some telegrams. However, there's nothing to stop the bride's father or the groom opening something like this:

Ladies and Gentlemen,
before I start, I've been asked to make the
following announcements;

Will the owner of Toupee, Serial number
727318, kindly collect it from the foyer ...
it's beginning to confuse the cat!

I have good news and bad news ...
first the good news ...
After the speeches, the bride's uncle Stanley
will be giving us all a song ...
That was the good news ...
and that'll give you some idea of how bad the
bad news is!

By the way, Stanley will be singing that lovely
standard; "I'm dancing tonight with tears in
my eyes, 'cos the girl in my arms is a boy".

Ladies and gentlemen,
we're all here today because ...

... and you're into the speech.

People are now quite used to seeing you glancing down at the paper, and, as long as you bring your head up and look around the room regularly as you speak, they won't be conscious of you reading from a script.

By the way, during your speech, always make sure your next page is ready for you well before you come to the end of your current page.

## *Hello Mike!*

You'll be reading from a full script, so you'll need both hands available throughout your speech. One hand will be holding the paper, the other will need to be free for page-turning, gestures, water-sipping, toasting or – should you insult the wrong guy – **self-defence.**

It's almost essential, therefore, to ensure that you have a free-standing microphone. I prefer a table-stand, but any mike-stand will do. You'll have to arrange for this in advance. Don't trust it to luck and **don't** believe people who tell you to leave it all to them ... it's **your** responsibility ... **you're** the one who'll look awkward if things are not right.

Don't test the mike by blowing on it or saying; "One two, one two!" ... if you do, I'll come over there and knock your bloody block off **myself!** Right?
Just tap the mike gently to make sure it's working. If it's not, get someone to switch it on.

Speak from the table if you can, not from the stage. The stage becomes a barrier between you and the audience and interferes with that special intimate relationship. Instead of speaking as part of the crowd, the platform or dance floor makes it a case of 'us and them' and you won't get the results your material deserves.

When you speak, speak loudly, speak clearly and speak with confidence. After all, you can afford to speak with confidence when your material is strong, and it **will** be ... stick around.

# Material

Try to use totally original gags; it doesn't matter where you steal them from. After all, the line between 'inspired by' and 'nicked from' is a very fine one.

As you will have gathered by the originality demonstrated in this book, I don't **need** to nick anything. When I do, it's for the pure joy of larceny. However, as I invented so much of this material myself, I have a request -
If one day, you happen to find that we're both speaking at the same function, please exercise some professional etiquette; steal from Bob Monkhouse's book instead.

You get extra points with an audience if your material is, or sounds, original. If you personalise your one-liners accurately enough, you may well create that illusion. You also get extra points for topicality. What's the big news story on the day of the wedding? Can you adapt a line cleverly enough to refer to it?
No?
Oh.
Tough!

# HOW TO USE 'ROAST LINES' AND INSULTS

The important thing to remember about 'roast' material is that it has to have a ring of truth about it in order to be funny. These jokes are verbal caricatures. They take a defect or a quirk and exaggerate it. If the bridegroom is a little – how can I put it? – careful with money, the best man may well say;

> **Some men marry for love,**
> **some men marry for companionship . . .**
> **Dave needed a new toaster!**

If the bride recently had an accident in the kitchen and called it "dinner", her father may have to admit that he's going to miss her cooking . . . as often as he can! Even the thought of her mashed potatoes gives him a lump in his throat!

However, if the bridegroom is known to be extravagant and the bride is a Cordon Bleu cook, the lines are meaningless.

Whatever you do, don't contrive a situation or a characteristic in order to justify using a one-liner, no matter how funny you think it is. Try to hit the button, but don't be **too** cruel. Even if the roastee is liable to take it well, many members of the audience are going to be concerned for your victim's feelings if you cross that sensitive line.

Think about the person you wish to rib; you may find something in his (never **her**) appearance – shortish, balding, beer belly? Is he a lousy golfer? A lazy bugger? A wimp? I hope so. All that makes for a much better speech.

# GOOD TASTE

These days, a wedding speech needn't be 'squeaky clean' but you must use some common sense. Learn the art of stopping before offence . . .
just like that good-for-nothing horse I used to own.
Select every one-liner with great care – especially the ones in this book. If in doubt; leave it out. (Poetry's a piece of cake, isn't it?)

Know your customers. Judge how broadminded the crowd is liable to be. Will members of the clergy be present? Is there a strait-laced maiden aunt around? It wouldn't hurt to check things out.

I discussed this whole question with the Right Reverend Noel Jones, Bishop of Sodor and Man. He feels that members of the clergy are not your problem; these days, churchmen are much more broadminded than people give them credit for. Beware, however, of certain guests . . . the old colonel uncle, the ancient aunt . . . A wedding is, after all, a **family** occasion with guests ranging from grandmothers to young tearaways through to little children. "It's best", said the Bishop, "to tread the middle path of safety. You'll almost certainly get away with near-the-mark references to the forthcoming honeymoon, complete with all the sexual innuendoes. This is expected and nobody is going to be too shocked.". As an example, he quoted the old evergreen; "The bride and groom won't be

long; they're upstairs, putting their things together!".
However, Bishop Jones felt that "deep vulgarity", is
unnecessary and will probably offend. "Bear in mind", he
said, "that at a wedding, many members of the two
families are meeting for the first time. What you say in
your speech may well play a part in the opinion formed by
one family towards the other."

I'm grateful to the Bishop for his advice and guidance on
this subject; it's valuable to have his opinion as one of
Britain's religious leaders.

Nowadays, as I've shown, you **can** get away with fairly
risqué material, but never be too vulgar; avoid being
'lavatorial' and try to be subtle with sexual references.

For normal wedding receptions, the serious four-letter
words are definitely taboo, of course. However, provided
you use them only occasionally and advisedly, words like
"pissed", "bullshit", "crap", are alright in the correct
context. (Out of context, they'll sound as stark as they did
in the previous sentence, so watch it!)

Over the years, as a speech-writer and a speech-maker,
I've learned that a well-written humorous speech which
manages to avoid vulgarity will win you respect from an
audience. This will enhance your image and up your
reputation. Nearly every client of mine has upped **his**
reputation ... up **yours**!

# CLICHÉS

I'm tempted to say "Avoid clichés like the plague!", but that would be a cheap and facile gag and therefore perfectly suitable for this book.

The real difficulty with clichés is that, by their very nature, they have become so much a part of the language it's easy to forget they're being used, so at least try to be conscious of them.

Of course, to be fair on these hackneyed phrases, they wouldn't have **become** clichés had they not been expressive and appropriate in the first place. However, their original meanings have often become obscured and, worse — people get them wrong.

You've heard the expression; "Laughing all the way to the bank!". Well, you shouldn't have done! The correct phrase is "**Crying** all the way to the bank!". So there!

The line seems to have been invented by Liberace and used in his autobiography. He wrote; "When the reviews are bad, I tell my staff that they can join me as I cry all the way to the bank.".

To fill a speech or even a conversation with trite banalities and stereotypical phrases, merely drives people into the clutches of professional writers like me. So keep it up.

# Content and Style

It's time for the first of our one-liners . . .

---

## OPENERS

---

A few ideas designed to grab an early giggle.

Family and friends . . .
I <u>would</u> call you "Ladies and gentlemen", but
I happen to know better.

Ladies and gentlemen,
it's been such an exciting day that I'm
absolutely speechless . . .
which is probably very good news for most of you.

Ladies and gentlemen,
before I begin . . .
Marks and Spencer have asked me to
announce . . .
that this . . .
is a C&A suit.

Ladies and gentlemen,
In the interests of being 'politically correct',
I've removed any controversial material from
this speech . . .
(pause) . . .
Thank you very much and good afternoon.
(Make as if to sit down.)

Ladies and gentlemen,
what I have to say today may well bring a
smile to your throat and a lump to your lips.

Ladies and gentlemen,
your host and hostess have requested that, for
reasons of safety, at the end of this speech you
refrain from getting up on the tables or chairs
during my standing ovation.
Thank you.

Ladies and gentlemen,
I've been asked to say a few words,
so here goes . . .
cornstarch . . .
oxyacetalene . . .
onomatopoeia . . .
and now for the speech . . .

Ladies and gentlemen,
I'm so happy and excited, I can hardly wait to
hear what I've got to say.

Ladies and gentlemen,
This is my A.B.C.D. speech . . .
above and beyond the call of duty.

Ladies and gentlemen,
this is the moment you've all been waiting
for . . .
and there it goes!


Ladies and gentlemen,
I'm delighted to have been asked to make this
speech today . . .
I've been dying to get out of that bloody
house.


Ladies and gentlemen,
I'm only going to speak for a couple of
minutes because of my throat . . .
if I go on too long, Elayne has
threatened to cut it.


Family and friends . . .
I'd like to admit straight away that I was a
little nervous earlier on, but happily I'm
feeling much better . . .
I'm completely at my ease now because, after
all, I realise I'm in front of my own kind of
people . . .
Drunks!

(You may substitute "Piss artistes" if you feel you can get
away with it; it'll get a bigger laugh.)

# FATHER OF THE BRIDE

STOP!
IF YOU HAVE JUST ARRIVED
DIRECT FROM PAGE TEN,
BEFORE ATTEMPTING TO READ THIS CHAPTER,
DO YOURSELF A FAVOUR –
RETURN TO PAGE ELEVEN

In any speech, it can be quite difficult to maintain the balance between being a gushing, sentimental old softie and a cold fish. This tends to be more of a problem when it comes to the speech made by the father of the bride. He needs to let his guests and family know how much he cares for his little darling, yet, if he uses the sincere language of a loving father, his audience is liable to start throwing up en masse.

You see, sincerity is not enough.

I know many **genuine** people who just can't help sounding like phonies; it's the language they use and the tone they adopt. To alleviate the 'O.T.T.' effect, avoid being too nice for too long. Alternate your sincere observations with little bits of humour. I call this style – 'Ping-pong'.

Here's a format which should give you an idea of what I'm getting at. This is not exactly a speech, these lines are the building blocks; you will need to add a few more words of thanks (don't forget the bride's mother), select some more one-liners and link them together to maintain the 'Ping-pong' effect.

Bride and bridegroom, family and friends,
ladies and gentlemen,
This won't be a long speech;
I don't have that large a vocabulary.

I'd like to thank you all for coming . . .
especially those of you who knew I'd be
saying a few words but turned up
nevertheless.

Some of you have travelled considerable
distances in order to share this happy day
with us . . . we have guests here from all over
the world; New Zealand, Mombassa,
Manitoba . . . these are the only three places
not represented here this afternoon.

So we greet you all with added pleasure and
our sincere appreciation for the trouble
you've taken to be here . . .
for you, drinks are half price!

Ladies and gentlemen,
there's something very special about a
wedding that we often overlook . . .
it's a unique opportunity for two families and
friends of those families to start getting to
know each other.
Of course, sometimes that's asking for trouble . . .
but in this case I must say, I don't think we'll
have any problems . . .
our two families now have a common bond
and I'm delighted to be sharing the day with
Janice and Allen - my daughter's new in-laws.
I also look forward to sharing with them, the
future pleasures which will, no doubt, come
to us through Lucy and Dave.

It's inevitable, I suppose, that a day like today inspires a few memories . . . in particular, memories of this young bride's formative years.

You know, when Lucille was born, she looked exactly like me . . .
then they turned her the right way up and all was well.

People think of my daughter as a very bright young lady, and so she is . . .
but we weren't too sure when she was younger . . .
at kindergarten, Lucy was different from all the other five year olds . . .
she was eleven!

And I have to admit that even at Victoria College she was not the brightest of pupils . . .
one day in the assembly hall she saw a sign saying: 'WET FLOOR' . . . so she did!

At one stage, I had my doubts about the crowd she was hanging around with . . .
I used to have to pay her pocket money in unmarked bills!

But our Lucy was never any trouble at home. She was a quiet girl. Every now and then, I'd glance up at the shelf and there she'd be . . .
waiting . . .

Thankfully, today marks the end of that waiting and I know that Lucy feels that Dave has been well worth waiting for. He is, after all, a fine young man with many interests . . . he's into sailing and golf and, so far, his progress in the world of business has been meteoric. I'm confident that my daughter is in good hands; after all, show me a man with both feet on the ground, and I'll show you a man who . . . can't put his trousers on!

Dave, you certainly seem to know how to make Lucy happy and I'm quite sure you'll continue to do so.

Welcome to the family . . .
and believe me, you <u>are</u> welcome to the bloody family!

I think you'll find that Lucy is going to be an asset to you in all sorts of ways . . .

She's quite a career girl herself and, even though a father shouldn't really say it, Lucille has everything it takes to be a success in business . . .
a quiet charm, a persuasive manner, the ability to grovel without laddering her tights . . .

But Elayne and I are very proud parents today . . .
I'm sure you'll all agree that Lucy looks absolutely stunning this afternoon . . .
and the nice thing is, she's as lovely on the inside as she is on the outside . . .
(Pause for "Hear hears")

Lucy and Dave . . .
marriage is a great university. It teaches you
patience, consideration, understanding . . .
and all sorts of crap you wouldn't even need if
you stayed <u>single</u>!

I'm totally confident that the two of you will
graduate with honours.

Ladies and gentlemen,
please join us in drinking a toast to the happy
couple, Lucy and Dave . . .
I know you're going to be great together . . .
God bless you and good luck to you both!
(Raise glass)

See what I mean? First sweet, then zap! First this way, then
that. Ping-pong.

By the way, another good thing about the Ping-pong
method is that the audience doesn't want to miss the next
one-liner, so they actually concentrate . . . in much the
same way as you can't put this book down because I'm so
bloody hilarious!

## *Extra Lines Suitable for the Father of the Bride*

In addition to 'roast' lines and other zingers elsewhere in this book, the following may be specifically useful.

My function today is simple; to give away the bride. Of course, after paying for all this lot, the bride is all I have left <u>to</u> give away!
> (Bridging Line)

Lucy is our only child . . .
after she was born, we decided to stop while we still outnumbered her.

She ran away from home once, but for three days nobody missed her . . .
we all thought she was still in the bathroom!

She was always a good girl . . .
in fact she's got so used to saying "no", she nearly screwed up the wedding ceremony!

I'm going to miss her, but let's face it, she's not getting married one day too soon . . .
they've been together for eight years. Eight years! Come to think of it, instead of the Wedding March I should have got the organist to play the Hallelujah Chorus!

This morning, my sin-in-law became my son-in-law.

Living together without being married is like being punished for a crime you didn't commit!


When Dave first approached me and said;
"I've come to ask for your daughter's
hand" . . .
I told him; "It's alright with me, as long as
you take the one that's always in my pocket!".
"No", he said, "You don't understand . . .
I want your daughter for my wife!"
I said; "What would your <u>wife</u> do with her?".


I've come to think of Dave as I do my own
son . . .
the one I threw out of the house and
disowned.


My daughter really likes the good things
in life . . .
I don't know if you overheard this, but
earlier, when the vicar asked if there were any
objections, Lucy said; "Yeah! What's all that
crap about 'for richer or for poorer'?!".


I was so proud to see her today as she swept
down the aisle . . .
Believe me Buster, that's the last time you're
ever going to see <u>her</u> sweep!

(Bridging Line)

Elayne and I really hope that Lucy and Dave are going to make grandparents of us.
Of course it's their decision, but I must say that people with no children are really missing out ... they'll never know what a thrill it is to come home after a hard day, sit down to a hot dinner and watch someone stuffing spaghetti hoops up their nose!


Kids are crucial to family life ...
without them, how the hell would we ever be able to programme a video recorder?!


Lucy and Dave are marrying in their early twenties because they want their children young. Quite right. After all, who wants old children?

You may wish to incorporate into your speech, a quotation on this subject of marriage. Don't use more than one or two. You'll find some near the end of this book.

## FATHER'S ADVICE TO THE BRIDE AND BRIDEGROOM


As the two of you go forward hand in hand into the big, wide world ...
I can do no better than to offer you some of the advice that has been passed down in our family from generation to generation ...
and never used.

There are three things you must remember to give during a marriage; inspiration, income, in.

The best way to make sure you always remember your wedding anniversary is to forget it just once.

Make it a point never to argue about anything not worth arguing about.
But be careful; sometimes you can get into a fight trying to decide what's worth arguing about!

Live each day as if it were your last, and each night as if it were your first.

Let your bride know who's boss right from the start . . .
there's no point trying to fool yourself!

## TAKE MY WIFE . . . PLEASE!

If – and only if – the new mother-in-law is a good sport, these lines are for the new father-in-law . . .

Elayne and I have been married twenty-seven years. . . honestly, it seems like yesterday . . .
and you know what a lousy day yesterday was!

Speaking for myself, I simply couldn't imagine being single again . . .
at least not without getting a silly grin on my face!

In all that time neither of us has even
<u>considered</u> divorce . . .
Homicide, but never divorce.

But I just <u>love</u> being married . . .
especially those quiet times apart!

As you know, a 25th Wedding Anniversary is
Silver . . . A 50th Anniversary is Gold.
<u>Our</u> next anniversary is . . .
Shrapnel!

Since we were married,
I never looked at another woman;
she put me right off 'em!

I never kept any secrets from my wife . . .
I tried, but I never could.

On our tenth anniversary, we revisited the
hotel we went to for our honeymoon . . .
this time, <u>I</u> ran into the bathroom and cried!

You know, Elayne believes that I'm the
world's greatest lover . . .
but she's never quite managed to catch me at it!

We've shared the same bed for twenty-seven
years . . .
She sleeps in it at night -
I take the day shift.

I've been very depressed lately;
my wife has been threatening to leave me . . .
even that hasn't cheered me up!


I never knew what true happiness was until I
got married and then . . .
it was too bloody late!


We have a sign at home;
'Views expressed by husbands are not
necessarily those of the management.'.


I saw a girl in Playboy who measured
39-24-35 and I finally figured out what's
wrong with my wife . . .
she's inside out!

## THE COOK

The following lines are, on the face of it, directed at
females. Most of them may easily be adapted to knock the
male cook. I'm not being sexist, honest.
Anyway what if I am?


I hate to say it, but she's not a very good cook . . .
we had people over for dinner two weeks ago
and they're still sitting there!


She used to dress to kill . . .
now she just cooks that way.

Her cooking leaves a little to be desired . . .
namely - taste!

There are two reasons why husbands leave
home; wives who <u>can</u> cook and won't,
and wives who <u>can't</u> cook and do.

For the last six weeks she served up chicken
every Thursday . . .
What d'you mean "What's wrong with that?"
- it was the same chicken!

She's such a bad cook,
she won't lick her own fingers!

I had a feeling there was something wrong
from day one when I got up, walked into the
kitchen and found her ironing the bacon!

The recipe called for a little flour,
so she threw in a tulip.

I came home once to find she'd left me a note;
'Dinner's in the cookery book, page 14.'.

When the dish ran away with the spoon, they
were escaping from her kitchen.

You've got to give her some credit for being
inventive . . .
Who else would have come up with 'Soup In
A Basket'?!

My job, when she's about to start cooking,
is to go from room to room,
removing batteries from the smoke alarms.


I remember the day she baked a coconut pie
... how she got the pie into that coconut, I've
no idea!


Most days there'd be a line of pygmies outside
the kitchen window, queueing up to dip their
arrows in her soup.


Lately she's been cooking so much fish,
I've started breathing through my cheeks!


Her specialities include;
'Avocado You'll Regret', 'Smoked Salmonella',
'Boeuf Beenangorne', 'Hash Black Potatoes'.


She spends all her time in the kitchen.
She's always baking, baking, baking ...
now that wouldn't be so bad, but - salads?!


People are always asking her for her recipes ...
I suppose they're hoping she'll give away her
only copy.


She specialises in Cajun cookery ...
every morning she makes blackened toast.

# THE BRIDEGROOM

STOP!
IF YOU HAVE JUST ARRIVED
DIRECT FROM PAGE TEN,
BEFORE ATTEMPTING TO READ THIS CHAPTER,
DO YOURSELF A FAVOUR –
RETURN TO PAGE ELEVEN

In my opinion, the bridegroom's speech – for all the reasons I gave earlier – is the most difficult to pitch exactly right. He'll be speaking in front of his new in-laws and their guests, his bride (probably still somewhat bonded to Mummy and Daddy), his own family and his leering, drunken, mickey-taking friends.
What's called for is a clever balancing trick.
Let me refer you to the 'Ping-pong' technique I wrote about at the beginning and end of the previous section devoted to the Father of the Bride. The groom may find this cheap trick equally useful.

In his speech, the bridegroom – speaking also on behalf of his bride – should begin by responding to the toast made by his new father-in-law. He may wish to thank his in-laws for their hospitality (if applicable), and his own parents for all their help and support over the years.

At this point, his eyes begin to fill with tears as he tells everyone how lucky he is to have found his bride. (I suggest a little raw onion hidden behind the nail of the index finger.)

He thanks all his friends and family for coming along, shows gratitude for the generous wedding gifts, compliments the ushers on doing a fine job, mentions how beautiful the bridesmaids are (by the way, be careful; it's not easy to hold a champagne glass with your fingers crossed) and winds up by proposing a toast to them.

All very nice, but where's the bite?

One thing's for certain, when the best man starts to speak, the bridegroom is really going to have to put up with some put-downs.

My advice is ATTACK!
Go for a pre-emptive strike.

Bring the best man into your speech, thank him for all he's done to help make the day a success, then . . . pluck his feathers out one by one!

Like the sample text I used for the bride's father, the following sequence is not exactly a speech, these lines are merely the building blocks; you will need to personalise them and to expand them as necessary.

When insulting the best man, think of his weaknesses and his peculiarities and choose some appropriate lines. Don't forget, these are spoken caricatures . . . just exaggerate the truth.

If there are no bridesmaids involved, it may be nice to close the speech with a toast to your new bride. Choose one from the 'Toasts' section.

Host and hostess, family and friends, ladies
and gentlemen;

Today, you are looking at a very happy man . . .
and I wish you'd turn round and look at me
instead, because I'm trying to make a speech!

Firstly, I'd like to thank my new father-in-
law, Jack Lucas, for his kind words.
It's amazing what some people will say when
they're not under oath.

Of course this is a very important day for me
- second only to my stag night - so I'm sure
you'll understand if I seem to be a little
nervous . . . it's only natural . . .
marriage is, after all, a pretty big step . . .
and these days, you've really got to be careful
what you step into!

I must say we've had some very nice wedding
presents and Lucy joins me in thanking you
for your generosity . . .
as a matter of fact, we're beginning to regret
that we didn't have an engagement party.
But of course, the 'presents' that we're really
thrilled about . . . is your presence here
on this very special day.
It's wonderful to see you all.

Thank you Jack and Elayne, not only for
your superb hospitality this evening and
for your many kindnesses, but also for giving
me your beautiful daughter.
I promise I'll take good care of her and I'll
always try to make her happy.

Like Lucy, I was lucky enough to be brought
up in an enlightened, well-balanced and
loving atmosphere by two terrific parents.
My Mum and Dad are remarkable people . . .
they taught me so much and gave me solid-
gold advice, leadership and love.
You know, Dad was always a wonderful
provider and a hard-working man . . .
he used to get up at 5.30 am to do nineteen
hours of strenuous work and thought nothing
of it! . . .
as it happens, I'm very much the same . . .
I don't think much of it either!!
I'm delighted that Mum and Dad are with us
today, helping us both to enjoy the happiness
of this occasion. It gives me an opportunity,
publicly, to thank them for everything they've
done in guiding and shaping my life.
Thank you Mum and Dad.

You know, I married this young lady because,
quite frankly, only the best will do for
Newberry.
You see, I've always been very fussy . . .
at one time, I was looking for a girl who
didn't smoke, didn't drink, wasn't interested
in The Chippendales and didn't keep asking
for money for clothes . . .
When I finally found one, she was <u>nine</u>!

Now don't get me wrong . . .
I've had my wild moments . . .
There was a time in my early twenties when I
really began living the life of Riley . . .
Then one day, Riley came home earlier than
usual and I had to make a run for it!

But a man can't carry on like that forever . . .
for medical reasons more than anything else.
In any case, society <u>resents</u> that much
happiness.

Well, POO to society 'cos I found something a
lot better, and today my Lucy promised to
devote herself to loving me until the end of
time . . .
Or 'Newsweek', whichever subscription
expires first!

Of course, this is a girl with many wonderful
qualities . . . anyone who knows her will
understand why I consider myself a very lucky
man today.
Mind you, her time-keeping leaves a lot to be
desired . . .
She's <u>always</u> late . . .
In fact, British Midland have just named a
delayed flight in her honour!

I would like to say, however, that she's really
excellent around the home . . .
I really <u>would</u> like to say that . . .
Wish I could.
You know, Lucy was trying to bake a cake
recently and the recipe said:
'Separate two eggs' . . .
so she put one in the living room and one in
the hall!
She'll catch on.

But I really couldn't ask for a better
woman . . .
if I did, she'd kill me!
Mind you, after this speech, she's probably
going to kill me anyway!

In case some of you were wondering, let me
put your minds at rest . . .
there's no possible way I was going to forget
to mention the four brave survivors from my
stag party . . .
Thank you Richard, Keith and John for acting
as ushers this morning . . .
and for getting it right! . . .
I'm impressed.

As for Andy, besides being my brother, he's
also my greatest friend and I'm proud to have
him as my best man . . .
not that he's going to get the chance to prove
that tonight!
You know, they say that blood is thicker than
water . . .
Andy Newberry is thicker than both.
It really is impossible to praise this guy too
highly . . .
it's impossible to praise him at all . . .
he's crap!
And yet, ladies and gentlemen, as you get to
know him, Andy will begin to have an effect
on you . . .
He'll creep into your heart . . .
He'll creep into your mind . . .
He'll creep into your soul . . .
He's the biggest creep in town!
But he's our creep!

By the way, Channel Four is planning a
documentary based on his sex life . . .
it's called; 'Sixty Seconds'.

He'll be getting up to speak in a moment or two, and he has some really unusual material today . . . his suit!
So I suppose I'd better make way now and give him a chance.

Ladies and gentlemen,
this is the happiest day of my entire life, and I really must thank Lucy for pointing that out to me.

We've had a really wonderful day . . .
starting at St. Matthews and continuing here with a delicious meal . . .
By the way, my compliments to the microwave . . .

Thank you all for giving us so much pleasure by sharing our wedding day with us.
Now, will you please join me in drinking the traditional toast to our gorgeous bridesmaids; Laura, Trudy and Angela . . .
and to Christopher, our macho pageboy.
Good luck and thank you for everything.
Cheers. (Raise glass)

## EXTRA LINES SUITABLE FOR THE BRIDEGROOM

In addition to 'roast' lines and other zingers elsewhere in this book, the following may be specifically useful.

I had to work very hard on this speech; it's too easy to make embarrassing mistakes . . .
like the one my friend Simon made when he thanked his in-laws for giving him a perky copulator!

When I went to my boss and asked him for a
raise, at first he turned me down.
He said; "I know you can't get married on
what I pay you and some day you'll thank me!".


My boss asked me how much time off I'd like
for the honeymoon . . .
I said; "Very nice of you, what do you
suggest?".
He said; "I don't know, I haven't seen the
bride.".


You know, I was in a position to marry
anyone I pleased . . .
Unfortunately, I didn't seem to please anyone.


You know, the first time I set eyes on Lucy, I
was immediately struck by her looks . . .
to me, she was "drop-dead gorgeous!" . . .
I said "You're gorgeous!" . . .
she said "Drop dead!".


From the very beginning she had me eating
out of her hand;
it certainly saved a lot of washing up!


When I first started going out with Lucy, it
was only natural that I should take her home
to meet my parents . . .
of course, they liked Lucy immediately - they
took to her straight away . . .
trouble was, they didn't approve of <u>me</u>!

Andy is a very talented man.
Very talented indeed . . .
He's a gifted designer, a shrewd entrepreneur,
a witty raconteur, a deep thinker and a
sensitive, caring one-woman man.
Andy is so talented, he can <u>fake</u> all of that!

You know, in life we sometimes take things
for granted . . .
For instance, I never realised just how much I
owed to my father . . .
until he foreclosed on my house.

You may wish to incorporate into your speech, a
quotation on the subject of marriage. Don't use more than
one or two. You'll find some near the end of this book.

The one-liners continue . . .

## BALDING

It's great to see him letting his hair down . . .
it's only fair,
lately his hair's been letting <u>him</u> down.

He used to have nice wavy hair,
but then one day, it waved "bye bye" . . .
it was a sad parting.

His hair has turned prematurely gone.

He's thinking of going to Africa
to find his roots.

He keeps his hat on with a suction cap.

If there were such a thing as a hair fairy,
he'd be a wealthy man today.

He used to have a crew cut, but the crew
bailed out.

Andy ... good news. There's a wonderful new
treatment for baldness on the market;
it doesn't grow hair ...
it shrinks your head to fit what hair you have left!

## THE CHURCH AND THE DREADED CLERGY

*The Church:* The first time you go,
they throw water on you ...

The second time you go,
they throw rice on you ...

The third time you go,
they throw earth on you.

I asked the vicar if he believed in sex before
the wedding.
He said: "Not if it delays the ceremony.".

By the way, the vicar has asked me to point
out that his church accepts all denominations;
fivers, tenners, fifties ...

Did you notice, he's put a sign up outside the
church; 'Keep off the grass.
This means <u>thou</u>!'.

Of course there's life after death;
you don't think we get off <u>that</u> easy do you?

The story of Adam and Eve makes you think,
doesn't it?
Adam didn't <u>have</u> a mother-in-law . . .
and he lived in paradise.

Here's a man who followed the Ten
Commandments all his life . . .
Never caught <u>up</u> with any of them, but . . .

In the words of J.C. Crawford -
the naughty vicar of Branfield -
"Well what did you expect?
I <u>am</u> a missionary!".

## SILLY STUFF

This is just a smattering of daft bits and pieces. Who
knows? One of them may just fit the bill.

She tried to kill him with a look, but she was
cross-eyed, so she killed another man.

He once joined a girl to forget the Foreign Legion.

She couldn't make it today;
she's got a part-time job at the stables
and her work is piling up.

He used to wake himself up with his snoring.
Not any more . . .
now he sleeps in another room!

He looked very distinguished standing there
with a pipe in his mouth . . .
but then he started blowing bubbles.

He's a very strange guy;
I saw him last week, walking his goose!

This is a man who doesn't know what he
wants . . .
and is willing to go through <u>hell</u> . . . to get it!

When he was a kid, his mother used to say;
"Stop biting your nails! . . .
or at least, put your shoes back on when
you've finished!".

I couldn't find any alphabet soup at Tesco's
on Saturday . . .
It must be out of print.

The first time he saw her swimming in the sea
he thought she was a girl worth wading for.

She's always on some kind of a diet.
There was one where she could only eat
waxed fruit . . .
one night, she broke into Madame Tussaud's
and binged on Julian Clarey!

At one point in his life, he fell in love with a
lady painter and decorator and was overcome
with emulsion.

He very nearly had a telepathic girlfriend once . . .
but she left him before they even met.

I'll never forget the first time I saw this character . . .
He was standing in the canteen all bleary
eyed, coffee in hand.
No cup, just coffee in his hand.

After he saw the film 'Roots',
he tried tracing his family,
but they refused to lie down on the paper.

Ladies and gentlemen,
yesterday I had a spell of deja vu . . .
Or am I having it now?

## THICK

He willed his brain to Medical Science.
Five years ago they came and picked it up.

They say a fool and his money are soon
parted . . .
I first met him when he was out looking for
his money.

I remember the time he discovered his tree of
knowledge . . .
it was a bonsai.

Here's a man who laughs at adversity . . .
especially if you ask him to spell it.

He saw a car parked outside his house with a
sign in the window saying; 'Neighbourhood
Watch'.
He kept tapping on the windscreen asking
what time it was.

He's always been thick;
when his mother was pregnant with him,
she was arrested for being a dope carrier.

This is a man who believes that marshmallows
are brain food . . .
and in his case, he's right.

When he used to go hitch-hiking,
he always set out early to avoid the traffic.

If you ask me,
I think he had his ears pierced too deep.

His brain scan read; 'Out to lunch'.

His heart is in the right place . . .
It's just his mind we can't find.

It would be quite wrong to call him an idiot
. . . he can clothe himself and perform simple
tasks, so technically; he's a <u>moron</u>.

(See also 'Naïve' and 'Put-downs'.)


## THE WOMANISER

Some of these lines are aimed at bachelors, some at
married guys with eyes. Don't roast the married ones on
this subject in front of their wives.
Trust me on this.

All women look alike to him . . .
fanciable!

He's had so much on the side,
he walks with a limp.

He loved her for her mind . . .
until he found out that sex was the farthest
thing from it!

He once got kicked in the face just for kissing
the bride . . .
Mind you, it <u>was</u> two years after the ceremony.

The first time I ever met him, he had a
beautiful woman on his arm . . .
best tattoo I ever saw.

He met his wife in a singles bar . . .
both of them were surprised.

As a lover . . . well, suffice it to say
the girls all call him 'Superman' . . .
he's faster than a speeding bullet!

There was one special girl I remember . . .
she really had something that hit him between
the eyes . . . a husband.

They used to teach the birds and the bees
about <u>him</u>!

Fussy? He'll go for anything with a shadow!

He believes in wine, women and so-long.

He's beginning to think it's time for him to
take a wife.
The only question is; whose?

He didn't say he was taking her to Florida,
he said he was going to Tampa with her!

# DEFINITIONS

*Baby*
- A bald head and a pair of lungs.

*Bachelor*
- A selfish, callous undeserving man who has cheated some worthy woman out of a profitable divorce.
- Footloose and fiancée free.
- A man who never makes the same mistake once.

*Courtship*
- The period during which a girl decides whether or not she can do any better.

*Divorce*
- When two people make a mistake and one person pays for it.

*Husband*
- A guy who smiled back once too often.
- What's left of a sweetheart after the nerve's been removed.

*Intuition*
- That certain something which tells a woman she's right ... whether she is or not.

*Marriage*
- A broken engagement.
- When deep, passionate love ripens into friendship.
- A rest period between romances.

*Pram*
- Last year's fun on wheels!

*Sex*
- The poor man's polo.

*Silly Game*
- One your wife can beat you at.

# THE BEST MAN

STOP!
IF YOU HAVE JUST ARRIVED
DIRECT FROM PAGE TEN,
BEFORE ATTEMPTING TO READ THIS CHAPTER,
DO YOURSELF A FAVOUR –
RETURN TO PAGE ELEVEN

As I said early in the book, the best man is expected to be the 'star of the show'. All too often, however, he is ill-equipped and ill-prepared. Sometimes, he's just ill.

By now, Mr Best Man, you should have learned enough to be able to give the guests a very pleasant surprise. If you've followed the guidelines, yours will stand out as a speech to remember – a wedding gift to the bride and groom and an entertainment for the crowd.

Let me remind you that you are officially replying to the groom on behalf of the bridesmaids. If there are no bridesmaids, I suggest that you regard yourself as speaking on behalf of the guests.

You may wish to tell the bridegroom's life story in some detail, ribbing him along the way. It's also quite nice to refer to news stories and world events which were taking place around the time of his birth. This technique helps to create interesting pictures in the minds of your audience and puts the bridegroom's life into a chronological perspective. A good source of this information is Longman's 'Chronicle Of The 20th Century'.
Don't make a meal of it. Your speech should only last around seven minutes, ten at the most.

In the following draft speech, I have cast the bridegroom's brother as best man. I find this to be the case in one in every three weddings.

Host and hostess, bride and bridegroom,
ladies and gentlemen;

It's time for <u>me</u> to make a speech now and,
quite frankly, there's not a whole lot you can
do about that.

Firstly, on behalf of the bridesmaids, I'd like
to thank the bridegroom for his kind words.
You know, I had a feeling it was going to be
difficult to follow a speech by my brother
David and I was quite right . . .
I couldn't follow a bloody <u>word</u> of it!

I have to tell you that to be asked to act as
best man today is a great privilege . . .
and <u>bloody</u> inconvenient!

This morning, at the ceremony, I think
everyone will agree . . .
the bride looked absolutely <u>stunning</u>! . . .
(Pause for "Hear hears" and possibly a ripple of
applause.)
The groom looked absolutely <u>stunned</u>!

Of course, there's no doubt, marriage is a
wonderful invention . . .
but then, of course, so was the low level
flushing cistern!

Now I'm probably in a better position than
most, to pay tribute to the groom ...
after all, he's almost like a brother to me ...
and I'm not going to stand up here this
afternoon and make cheap, obvious jokes
about Dave ...
let's face it, he deserves respect.

Dave Newberry is a man who knows where
he's going ...
and who knows where he's been ...
He just doesn't know where he <u>is</u>!

He once left a note on his office door ...
it said; 'Back in an hour' ...
When he got back after lunch,
he saw the sign and sat down to wait!

He's not with us.

I honestly don't know what the hell I'm going
to do without my big brother ...
and believe me, I just can't wait to find out!

But ladies and gentlemen, I've been asked
today to <u>praise</u> Dave, not to bury him ...
Mind you, I must say, the vote was bloody
close!

Dave has always been very fussy about his
appearance ...
Now it isn't easy being a slave to fashion
when one head is missing off your bunny
slippers ...
... but he does his best.

Today, we see before us a very presentable
looking guy, so it may surprise you to learn
that it wasn't always that way . . .

Dave was not a pretty baby . . .
mother didn't get morning sickness until <u>after</u>
he was born!

Yes, our parents were a little disappointed
when David came into the world . . .
they'd set their hearts on a golden retriever.

He was a slow starter . . .
at kindergarten, my brother was different
from all the other five year olds . . .
he was <u>eleven</u>!

By the time he was fourteen, Mum and Dad
were very concerned about his performance
at school . . .
he wasn't just falling behind,
he was getting <u>lapped</u>!
When friends asked them what they thought
Dave would be when he left school,
they used to say; "About thirty-five!".

My brother spent much of his teens trying to
find himself. Then, one fateful day, he had a
haircut . . . and there he was!

Happily, as we all know, the lovely Miss
Lucas came into his life and today, seeing
Dave with his wonderful bride, I realise what
a good choice he's made . . .
I really admire his taste . . .
which is more than I can say for <u>hers</u>!

Never mind, one thing's for sure . . .
with Lucy by his side, how can he possibly
go wrong?

Lucy has some remarkable qualities,
one of which - thank goodness -
is a well-developed sense of humour.
She'll need that for a start.
Of course, she'll also need quite a lot of
patience . . .

Dave has one rather disturbing habit; he tends
to keep putting things off. Yes, people have
often accused him of being a procrastinator . . .
one of these days I'm sure he'll get around to
denying it . . .
but he certainly didn't <u>dare</u> try to delay
today's ceremony . . .

After all, he of all people should know how
volatile Lucy can be. A few weeks ago, after a
little disagreement they had, I watched her
throw a pile of Dave's clothes straight out of
the window.
Trouble was, he was <u>wearing </u>them at the time!

Ladies and gentlemen,
it's now my pleasant duty to thank Dave on
behalf of the bridesmaids Laura, Trudy and
Angela, for his very kind words . . .
it's a real pleasure to act as spokesman for
such a lovely team of ladies . . .
I'd also like to add my thanks to Elayne and
Jack Lucas on behalf of all the guests for the
hospitality we've enjoyed this afternoon.
Like everybody here, I wish Lucy and Dave
all the happiness in the world.

As a man who'll drink to absolutely anything,
I'd be very grateful if you would all give me
an excuse to raise my glass again by joining
me in one more toast to the happy couple . . .
and this piece of advice to my big brother . . .
Dave . . .
"To keep your marriage brimming in the
everloving cup -
whenever you're wrong, admit it . . .
whenever you're right; <u>shut up!</u>".

Ladies and gentlemen . . .
the new Mr and Mrs Newberry . . .
Lucy and Dave!

## EXTRA LINES SUITABLE FOR THE BEST MAN

Should a couple embarking on marriage be
frank and earnest?
Or should one of them be a girl?

Show me a modern man who comes home
every evening, is greeted with smiles and
compliments, has his coat taken, his shoes
removed, pillows arranged for him, made to
feel comfortable and welcome in every way,
then is served a really delicious meal . . .
and I'll show you a modern man who lives in
a Japanese restaurant.

The bride wanted a very simple wedding, and
that's what she got . . .
starting with the bridegroom.

At the last wedding I went to, the bride was so
ugly, everybody kissed the groom!

But marriage isn't for everyone . . .
men, for instance.

It only takes a couple of words mumbled in
church and you're married.
It only takes a couple of words mumbled in
your sleep and you're divorced.

Sex is no reason to get married . . .
unless you've lost interest in it.

By the way, I have some bad news for you Dave . . .
One of the waiters just brought Lucy a couple
of aspirins.

Lucy wanted a formal wedding,
so her father painted the shot-gun white!

Bigamy is having one wife too many . . .
monogamy is usually the same.

They have a wedding album, a wedding
video, a wedding book . . .
the <u>Geneva Conference</u> didn't have coverage
that good!

Scientists have found a definite link between
marriage, sex and astrology . . .
if you've been married over twenty-five years,
sex happens once in a blue moon.

So now, Dave's career as a bachelor can be
summed up in one word . . . over!

You may wish to incorporate into your speech, a
quotation on the subject of marriage. Don't use more than
one or two. You'll find some near the end of this book.

## BEST MAN'S ADVICE TO THE BRIDE AND BRIDEGROOM

Hug and squeeze and kiss her daily . . .
and if her daily won't go along with it,
try the au pair!

By the way, the best time to do
the washing up is . . .
straight after she tells you to.

If you're clever,
you'll always have the last word.
If you're <u>really</u> clever, you won't use it.

Lucy; treat him like a dog -
three meals a day, plenty of affection
and a loose leash.

If he ever threatens to leave you,
hold out for a firm promise!

Dave; don't be complacent. Keep a look-out
for little telltale signs of trouble in your
relationship . . . like . . .
if you see the milkman wearing your socks.

I mean, you wouldn't want her having
headaches with another man would you?

No matter how she treats you, it's always a
good idea to try and look a little hurt.

Like Mickey Rooney, I feel it's a good idea to
get married early in the morning.
That way, if it doesn't work out, you haven't
wasted the whole day!


Every now and then, try a little tenderness . . .
Sprinkle some monosodium glutamate on your
beloved.


Never go to bed angry . . . stay up and fight!


I'll tell you how much point there is in
arguing with your wife . . .
have you ever tried blowing out a lightbulb?


Marriage is something you have to work at,
nurture, add to . . .
you know, like a compost heap!

(Bridging Line)


## THE BIG DRINKER

He's a drinker, but he's a happy drinker -
always laughing and shaking hands . . .
even when he's alone.


Just a few minutes ago the barman said to
him; "What would you like to drink; brandy,
gin, scotch, lager?"
He said; "Yes".

When I left him on his stag night,
he was in the middle of the High Street,
trying to roll up the white line.

Ladies and gentlemen,
your bridegroom is a man of vision;
sometimes blurred, sometimes double!

I told him that vodka is a slow poison.
He said; "I'm in no hurry.".

When he gave blood recently, his was the only
contribution with a head on it.

Here's the good news . . .
he's not drinking anymore.
Here's the bad news . . .
he's not drinking any less.

He does fifty push-ups a day . . .
not intentionally, he just falls down a lot.
                                    (Bridging Line)

He was caught by the police under the new
strict breathalyser rules . . .
not only did he have to blow into the bag,
he then had to twist it into the shape of a
kangaroo.

He was in a panic yesterday;
he lost the cork from his lunch.

When pink elephants get pissed,
they see <u>him</u>!


What a party! I watched him for twenty minutes,
trying to get a mini pizza into the CD player!


One weekend in London, he was found
putting pennies into a sewer and
looking up at Big Ben . . .
he thought he was weighing himself.

(Bridging Line)


He gets drunk on water . . .
as well as on land.


The doctors gave him some tests
and it turned out to be serious . . .
they found blood in his alcohol system.

(Bridging Line)


He gets pickled so often his nickname is
"Onions".


He's a talented amateur magician . . .
he can walk down the street and turn
into a pub.        (Bridging Line)


Fame at last . . .
he's in the latest edition of 'Booze Who'.

When he's drinking spirits,
there's no use giving him a chaser . . .
<u>nothing's</u> going to catch him.


He's always short of money. He can never
manage to make both ends meet . . .
he's too busy making one end drink.

(Bridging Line)


He only feels really fulfilled when he's really
filled full!


Currently, his favourite tipple is a trendy new
cocktail called 'Autumn Leaf' . . .
One sip and you change colour and fall to the
ground!


I'll never forget the day he dropped a bottle of
scotch on the floor . . .
I'd never seen so many splinters in a tongue!


What a man! . . .
I once saw him down two bottles of brandy
and not once did he stagger.
Stagger? . . . He couldn't even bloody move!


He doesn't really remember how
he met Lucy . . .
he just sobered up one morning
and there she was!

(Bridging Line)

Actually, he can't drink too much right now . . .
tonight's a big night and he doesn't want to
take the risk . . .
Rumour has it that he's like a load of
fireworks in November . . .
bloody useless after the fifth!      (Bridging Line)


If Dracula bit him in the neck, he'd get a
Bloody Mary!

## THE BORE

I **hate** bores; they insist on talking about themselves when
I want to talk about *ME!*

Here are some lines to roast 'em with . . .


He has that magic ability to light up a room . . .
as soon as he leaves it.


If you happen to see two guys together and
one of them looks really bored . . .
he's the other.


You can always tell when he's talking rubbish;
his lips are moving!


He recently came down with 24 hour flu . . .
even a virus can't stand him any longer than
that!

There's an old Chinese proverb;
"One picture is worth a thousand words." . . .
Dave Newberry never had that picture.


When you're in his company, believe me -
there's never a dull moment . . .
it lasts all the way through.


Is he a man of small calibre or just a big bore?


You know, if all the people who sat through
one of Dave's stories were lined up three feet
apart, they'd stretch . . .
That's it . . . they'd stretch.


I could really enjoy his conversation if it
weren't for two things . . .
my ears!


Not only does he encroach on your time,
he trespasses on eternity.


He'll be speaking next and I can assure you,
he's really on form . . .
Chloroform!


He's the sort of conversationalist who leaves
people gasping for <u>less</u>.


He never opens his mouth,
unless he has nothing to say.

He's a keen gardener;
he talks to his plants . . .
no wonder they droop - they're asleep!
(Bridging Line)

They say his mind wanders a bit,
but let's face it;
wouldn't yours if you were in that body?
(Bridging Line)

## GOD'S GIFT
### (The ego has landed)

This couple is bound to be happy . . .
they're both very much in love with the
bridegroom.

I can see it now . . .
every night, he'll take her in his arms, hold
her close . . .
and tell her how wonderful he is.

He thinks he's God's gift to women.
If that's true, God obviously does His
shopping at Woolworth's.

Some people marry for love . . .
some people marry for companionship . . .
Dave got married because he wanted to see his
name printed on little matchboxes.

He says that if there's such a thing as
reincarnation,
he's coming back as himself!

He told me he's a self-made man ...
naturally, I accepted his apology.

His prized possession is on his desk, inscribed;
'To the greatest guy I know' ...
and, let me tell you,
I've never seen a mirror so well polished!

At one time he wanted to join the Navy ...
He wanted to join the Navy to let the world
see <u>him</u>!

His three favourite forms of entertainment are
Radio, TV and mirrors.

He's so conceited, he sends his mother
congratulations on <u>his</u> birthday.

If this guy's on an ego trip,
he must be travelling very light!

It's just as well he's not wearing an open-neck
shirt tonight;
he's <u>covered</u> in love bites ...
all self-inflicted, of course.

But there's a lot to be said for
Dave Newberry ...
and he's usually the one that's saying it.

He certainly knows a good thing when he sees it . . .
in the mirror.


He never has an unkind word to say about
anyone . . .
mostly because he only talks about himself.


## THE HAPPY COUPLE

When the bride and bridegroom have been living together
for some time, the usual "new home", "new beginning",
"married bliss" crap doesn't work. Some of the following
lines may be a little more realistic. (Nevertheless, there's
also a bit of crap in case you need it.)


They're such a busy couple;
he's never found her in and she's never found
him out.


They've worked out a great way of settling
arguments;
he admits he's wrong,
and she admits she's right.


They're a fastidious couple;
Lucy's fast and Dave's hideous.


We have here, two good God-fearing people
who observe the Ten Commandments . . .
five each.

Of course they have their little scraps,
but never anything very serious ...
nothing three police sergeants and a couple of
paramedics can't sort out.


They go together like Teflon and Velcro.


I've been asked to deny the rumour that they
met when they were both having sex-change
operations.


Lucy and Dave share a sense of humour ...
they <u>have</u> to share it;
he hasn't got one of his own.


They have a pre-nuptial agreement ...
nothing complicated -
He's going to wash and she's going to dry.


He's a bit stupid and she's always
on a diet ...
That's why they'll stay together through thick
and thin.                                    (Bridging Line)


They married for better and for worse;
he couldn't have done better,
she couldn't have done worse.


So now, Dave is married to a wonderful person.
Unfortunately, Lucy's not that lucky.

He proposed to her on his hands and knees . . .
he had to, she was under the table at the time.

(Bridging Line)

Lucy and Dave have slightly different
priorities;
she wants their marriage to work
and he wants <u>her</u> to work.

They fix breakfast together;
she makes the toast and he scrapes it.

(Bridging Line)

## THE HONEYMOON

So off they go tomorrow for their honeymoon
in Marbella . . .
God knows how Dave's going to hold his
stomach in for two solid weeks.

(Bridging Line)

Why is it they're flying hundreds of miles to
get away from people just so they can spend
half their honeymoon writing out cards that
say; "Wish you were here."?

They're booked in to a place that's pretty
unusual for a Spanish hotel . . .
it's finished.

It's so far off the beaten track,
the crow doesn't even fly there.

I don't want to spoil it for them,
but I know that hotel.
It was mentioned in the Michelin Guide . . .
it said; "Don't!".

It's such a dump . . .
Kate Adie stands in front of it and pretends to
be giving live coverage from Bosnia.

I must tell you Lucy and Dave, in the
bathrooms, the walls are full of cracks . . .
mind you, you've probably heard most of
them.

Lucy's had a special sign made to hang on the
outside of their hotel bedroom door; 'Please
disturb!'.

## HYPOCHONDRIACS

When I think of Dave Newberry,
I think of champagne . . .
Every pain he has is a sham.

He's so full of penicillin,
every time he sneezes he cures someone.

I've got a great wedding present for him -
it costs £300 and comes in a chest . . .
pneumonia.

This is a very sick man
in a perfectly healthy body.

When he was a kid and his mother was trying
to get him to take a sweet,
she'd have to tell him it was medicine!


If the truth be known,
this guy's not stricken - he's chicken!


Wanna spoil his day?
Just tell him how healthy he looks.


He takes no chances;
he has an annual check-up every week.


It was very moving this morning in church . . .
Lucy recited her vows . . .
Dave recited his symptoms.

(Bridging Line)


He's the only guy I ever met who could tell
me exactly how many measles he had.


The way he starts whingeing when he gets a
little cold, there's no way of knowing whether
to call a doctor or a drama critic.

## I'M SINGLE – HA! HA!

For those of you who don't know,
I'm not actually married;
I just look this way because I've been ill!


I admit that as a bachelor I have no real idea
of what it feels like to be happily married . . .
But then, of course, nor do most husbands!


Being single means you don't have to leave a
party just as you're starting to have a good time.


I often think of marriage myself;
it keeps my mind off sex!


I had this beautiful Sicilian girlfriend once . . .
She had a face that could break your heart,
and an uncle who could break your legs.


She lived on the other side of the street,
but she finally came across.


I've never been married but I think I know
what it must be like;
I tried to get out of a book club once.


When I get married,
it's going to be the real thing – sex!

## INFURIATING AND AGGRESSIVE

Use these lines for the guy who quite enjoys being thought
of as tough, ruthless and nasty. More gentle insults may be
found under 'Put-downs (Various)'.

Ladies and gentlemen . . .
if there's anybody here his afternoon, who
feels strangely nervous and apprehensive, it's
probably because you just went and married
Dave Newberry.

Now, nobody knows what made
Mr Newberry so bloody infuriating,
but whatever it was, it worked!

He's so infuriating that, when he was fifteen
years old, his <u>parents</u> ran away from home.

He's so infuriating that, on a visit to Canada,
a load of baby seals got together and clubbed
<u>him</u>!

He's so infuriating that, when he went to
India, he became the only man in history ever
to be told to "bugger off!" . . .
by <u>Mother Theresa</u>.

I'm one of his oldest friends . . .
he can't <u>get</u> new ones.

He's been described as conceited, selfish,
arrogant and insensitive . . .
and, let's face it, a mother should know!

He's trouble! This is the yob who broke the
bottle of ketchup over Gorbachev's head.

His idea of fun is to sneak into Claridges and
put piranha fish in the finger bowls.

He's got a split personality . . .
and I don't like either of them.

People who have known him for some time
have formed their own support group.

Yes, there's only one Dave Newberry . . .
but then of course, there was only one
Hiroshima!

His personality is such that he can walk into
the room and immediately make strangers.

He hasn't got many faults,
but he makes the most of the ones he has.

I wouldn't say he's a prat,
but he'll certainly do until one comes along.

Still . . . he's a nice guy deep down . . .
and sometimes, that's where I wish he was.

## LAZY

Dave has never been the type to sit in the
office watching the clock,
waiting for half-past-five . . .
He leaves at <u>four</u>!


He's due to go into hospital shortly . . .
they have to remove something from his
backside . . .
a chair.


Around the office, this man is like God;
he's rarely seen, he's holier than thou, and if
he does anything it's considered a bloody
miracle!


He has this driving, insistent, irresistible,
aggressive compulsion to do absolutely
nothing.


His job means he's able to work eight hours
and sleep eight hours . . .
Trouble is, they're the same eight hours.


They tell me he had his window box paved over!


He says he's superstitious . . .
he won't do any work during a week that has
a Friday in it.

He's certainly not afraid of work . . .
he fights against it like a tiger!

He's a late riser; in fact, until recently he
didn't realise there were two eight o'clocks in
the same day.

## NAÏVE

He's always been rather naïve when it comes
to sexual matters -
he actually believes that mutual climax is an
insurance company!

She thinks Spanish Fly is something on the
front of King Juan Carlos's trousers.

He thinks the menopause is a control button
on a video recorder.

Someone told him the most important thing in
sex is foreplay, so he invited another couple.

She's a bit naïve when it comes to politics.
When I asked her opinion of Red China, she
said it looks best on a white tablecloth.

He's just as bad . . . when I asked him if he's
a right-winger or a left-winger . . .
he said he prefers the drumsticks.

# OCCUPATIONS

*Actor*    During the ceremony, he made it
very obvious he was an actor.
When the vicar said; "Do you
take this woman to be your
lawful wedded wife?" . . .
he paused, then whispered;
"Line?".


*Advertising*    The nice thing about the
advertising business is that it
really keeps you fit;
every lunch hour,
you're out looking for another
job.


*Architect*    He had designs on the boss's
wife.


*Boss*    He said; "The door to my office
is always open . . .
so keep your bloody voice down
as you go past!".


*Church*    He didn't make it as a priest . . .
he kept giggling during the last
rites.

| | |
|---|---|
| *Circus* | The whole show went to Birmingham in a specially chartered bus . . . all except the contortionist; he went under his own auspices. |
| *Dentist* | If a dentist breaks a dental mirror in your mouth, do you get seven years of bad teeth? |
| *Doctor* | She's so jealous, she listens in on his stethoscope. |
| *Electrician* | He made a fortune in Amsterdam . . . he was an electrician in the red-light district. |
| *Estate Agents* | Business was so quiet that he sat around most of the time, playing Monopoly with his partners, and guess what . . . none of the houses sold! |
| *Hairdressers* | She had to close up the business because she just couldn't make split ends meet. |
| *Law Student* | For a girl studying law, she didn't put up much of a defence. |

**Lawyer**  It's a mixed marriage . . .
He's a lawyer and she's a
human being.

**Musician**  He's technically fantastic!
He never hits a wrong note . . .
never makes a mistake . . .
it's amazing! . . .
all that crap is quite deliberate.

**Office Work** He's got so used to fax
machines, he can't read
anything unless it's curled up.

**Publishing** For a time, he worked for the
publisher of a thesaurus . . .
then, one day, he was fired,
canned, dismissed, let go,
dispensed with, discharged . . .

**Salesman**  For a time, he went round
door-to-door, selling "knock
knock" jokes.

**Undertaker** He learned his craft in
California, working for a
mortician whose slogan was;
"Have a nice death.".

# OVERWEIGHT

This guy has the body of a twenty year old ...
A twenty year old <u>Volvo!</u>

No man is an island ...
but Dave Newberry comes pretty close.

The poor bloke suffers from stomach trouble;
he can't get his trousers over it!

Actually, that isn't really his stomach ...
he's just got a low chest.

He used to be worse ...
at one point he got so fat,
his belly button unravelled itself.

He's got a sunken living room at home.
He didn't plan it that way, it just happened.

They say there are three men to every woman
in this town ...
Looks like Lucy got hers all in one lump.

Yes, at first glance he may look a little heavy,
but don't let that fool you;
he's quite capable of touching his toes ...
only with his belly, but it's a start!

(Bridging Line)

But he's in shape . . .
the <u>wrong</u> shape.


He weighs in at twelve-four . . .
on the Richter Scale!


The first time I met him, he was standing on
the corner of Oxford Street . . .
and Fulham High Road.


He does wonderful impressions . . .
he eats like a pig and drinks like a fish.

(Bridging Line)


He always used to say he was saving himself
for when the right girl came along . . .
did he have to save so much?


He claims to be a light eater. He is . . .
As soon as it gets light he starts eating!


As it happens, he's very conscious of his diet.
Every day he eats something from one of the
four main food groups . . .
McDonalds, Burger King, Wimpy and
Kentucky Fried Chicken!


Yes, for him a balanced meal means
a <u>Big Mac</u> in each hand!


His idea of pumping iron is lifting a knife,
fork and spoon!

(Bridging Line)

He's obsessed with food ...
this is a guy who always puts his stomach first;
especially when he's going through a door.


He hasn't an ounce of excess flesh
on his body ...
he's got <u>pounds</u> of it!


He got hit by a Lada once ...
it took three surgeons to remove it.


He's certainly got a good head on his
shoulders ...
mind you, it would look better on a <u>neck</u>.

(Bridging Line)


This guy's had more hot dinners ...
than you've had hot dinners.


He's so fat,
they've made him an honorary suburb.


He tried to run away from home once when
he was a kid,
but the fridge was too heavy.


This man is not only larger than life,
he's also larger than his own trousers.

(Bridging Line)

No wonder his stomach looks like a beer barrel . . .
it is!                                              (Bridging Line)

## PUT-DOWNS (VARIOUS)

He didn't get where he is today by luck . . .
he had to fight and claw his way to the
bottom.


Here's a man who started out with nothing . . .
and he still has most of it.


He may <u>seem</u> insignificant, but there's a lot
less to him than meets the eye.


Some people need no introduction . . .
Dave Newberry needs all the introduction he
can get.


Words cannot express my feelings for this man . . .
but <u>fingers</u> can!
(Make a 'V' sign towards victim.)


This man knows exactly where he's going . . .
and where he's been . . .
he just doesn't know where he <u>is</u>!


Look at him! . . .
maybe we can freeze him until we find a cure.

His father looks upon him as the son
he never had.


He's a man of hidden talents.
As soon as we find one, we'll let you know.


Dave Newberry could be described as
charming, intelligent and entertaining ...
and perhaps one day, he <u>will</u> be.


Nobody thinks more highly of him than I do,
and that'll give you some idea, 'cos I think
he's a prat!


He's a difficult man to forget,
but well worth the effort.


Here is a man who has taken dignity,
sound judgement and good taste ...
and thrown them right out of the window!


He's working on his second million ...
he gave up on his first.


When they made Dave Newberry,
they kept the mould and threw <u>him</u> away.


Some people are one in a million ...
Dave Newberry was won in a raffle.

He may <u>look</u> stupid,
but that doesn't mean he's not.

He seems too good to be true . . .
he isn't.

He's a man of hidden shallows.

Here's a guy who started his career at the
bottom . . .
and <u>stayed</u> there!

But he's unpredictable;
just as you begin to figure out what makes
him tick . . .
he begins to tock!

In business, he has a very sophisticated
technique for decision making . . .
"Eenie, meenie, miney, mo!".

Unfettered by ability, unhindered by style,
unimpeded by talent, this man is <u>above</u>
professionalism . . .
<u>he</u> is in a category of his own . . . crap.

He's bilingual . . .
unfortunately, neither language appears to be
English.

## *SHORT*

But I'm not going to stand up here and make
fun of my friend; life's too short . . .
and so is Dave.


The Newberrys are all the same . . .
his family tree is a <u>stump</u>!


You see, they just don't make guys like him
any longer.


He was offered a part-time job once . . .
standing around in a bar . . .
they reckoned he made the drinks look bigger.


He's very superstitious . . .
he thinks it's unlucky to walk under
a black cat.


He's a lumberjack . . .
For bonsai trees.

## SPORTS

**Bowling**     He's a tough guy . . .
when he goes ten pin bowling, he
bowls overarm.

**Boxing**     During his career, they threw the
towel in so many times,
he opened his own linen service.

**Cricket**     This all started when he was a
little boy and his father bought
him a bat for his birthday.
Imagine his surprise when he
unwrapped it . . .
and it flew away.

**Fishing**     Here's to our fisherman bold,
Here's to the fish he caught,
Here's to the one that got away . . .
And here's to the one he bought!

**Golf**     Ah yes! Give me some golf clubs,
some fresh air and a beautiful woman
. . . and you can <u>keep</u> the bloody
clubs and the fresh air!

**Motorsport**     His main hobby is drag racing . . .
and, let's face it, it isn't easy
jumping hurdles in a cocktail
dress!

**Parachute**     It's a tough sport . . .
**Jumping**     you jump out of a plane at fifteen
thousand feet, aim for a little
black dot on the ground and, if
you don't pull the ripcord on
time, that little black dot is you!

| | |
|---|---|
| *Referees* | You know the trouble with referees? ... they don't give a toss who wins! |
| *Rugby* | Playing rugger is a great way to meet new people ... Paramedics, nurses, orthopaedic surgeons ... |
| *Running* | I prefer sex ... it's much more fun and you don't need special shoes! |
| *Soccer* | The team is just like an old-fashioned bra ... no cups and poor support. |
| *Scuba Diving* | He had a narrow escape last year ... something went wrong and Jacques Cousteau's life passed before his eyes. |
| *Skiing* | Skiing's easy ... I learned in just ten sittings. |
| *Table Tennis* | The recreation room was so small, you couldn't even play 'ping-pong' ... all you could play was 'ping'. |
| *Tennis* | He has a service <u>no one</u> can return ... it always hits the net first! |

## THE WIMP

I feel confident Lucy will never leave him . . .
She's spent too much time training the poor
sod.


He's never been married before . . .
he's a self-made mouse.


Did you notice? When the vicar asked;
"Do you take this woman?", Lucy said;
"He does!".


He'll never forget the day he proposed to her . . .
it was the first time he's ever had his way of
kneeling criticised.


He's spent so much time buttering-up his
future father-in-law, he's developed
a cholesterol problem.


He's a mild, inoffensive man . . .
but then, of course, so was Crippen.


Poor bloke, even on his honeymoon
he's gonna have to play his cards right.


When he gets into a lift, he says;
"Fourth floor please . . . as long as it doesn't
take you out of your way.".

You know, he used to be a stunt man on
'Songs of Praise'.


He's very loyal in his relationships;
when he was a kid and he used to go out
walking with his mum, he never ever looked
at other mums.


Last year on holiday there was this bully on
the beach, trying to push him around . . .
He didn't take it lying down . . .
he got his own back on her grandchildren!

## THE OLDER MAN

A word of warning Lucy -
you'll have to make a few allowances.
At his age, his back goes out more often than
<u>he</u> does.


Don't be fooled by that healthy glow . . .
it's not a sun tan . . .
it's just that all his liver spots have grown
together.


Longevity runs in his family . . .
when his grandfather died, he was pushing a
hundred and three! . . .
Mind you, that was on the M6!


Have you heard about his drug habit? . . .
He snorts Phyllosan!


I'm looking forward to those long, summer
nights when we can all go over to their place
and sit round the table listening to the sound
of his arteries hardening.


I bet their first baby looks just like Dave . . .
all wrinkled and bald.

(Bridging Line)


He went to school in the days before History
was a subject.

After the speeches you may wish to shake the
bridegroom's hand,
but there's really no need . . .
at his age, just <u>hold</u> his hand and it'll shake
all by itself.

Despite his age, Dave Newberry has quite a
lot going . . .
His hair's going, his liver's going, his teeth
are going . . .

But really, he doesn't <u>look</u> forty . . .
not any more.

He still likes the good life, even at his age . . .
look at him, sitting there casually sipping his
pruna colada.

I know his blood type has been deleted from
the catalogue, but . . .

The three ages of men . . .
under age, over age and average.

## THE PREGNANT BRIDE

It happens a lot today. When the bride is pregnant, it's
usually pretty obvious to everyone anyway, so provided
folks are comfortable with the situation (especially the
bride), here are some lines . . .

This wedding proves once and for all that
opposites attract;
she's pregnant and he isn't.

It's been a typical love story;
at first she got his goat . . .
now she's carrying his kid!


I don't know if you noticed this but at the
ceremony, she didn't say "I do",
she said "I did"!


I really don't want to comment on just how
hastily this wedding took place, but why did
Nigel Mansell drive them to the church?


It's important that a newly-married couple are
able to make ends meet . . .
come to think of it, that's why they had to get
married.

(Bridging Line)


He proposed to her in a restaurant and it was
very sudden. Right out of the blue.
It was immediately after she ordered a
mushroom, pickle and chocolate pizza.


This was a shotgun wedding . . .
it made history; it's the first time the shotgun
was pointed at the woman!


By the way, let me read you an excerpt from
'Tips for First-time Parents';
Tip number 34; All newborn babies are
wrinkled. Do not try to iron them!

Remember; everything that goes into a baby's
mouth has to be boiled first . . .
Which probably explains why so few mothers
breast-feed.

Apparently, due to Health Service cuts, there's
a shortage of women who deliver babies . . .
a midwife crisis.

## THE SERIAL BRIDEGROOM

Here are some lines with which to rib the previously
married bridegroom. A word of warning; make sure the
bride is a good sport about his past and, in any case, don't
overdo it. Use two lines at the most.

Dave Newberry is a man who signs his
Wedding Certificate in pencil.

This guy's been up and down the aisle more
often than Oprah Winfrey!

His last marriage was like schoolwork;
When they met it was chemistry . . .
Then it turned to biology . . .
Now . . . it's history.

Some guys get married for money,
some guys get married for love . . .
this guy gets married for spite!

His top priority has always been finding the
right woman to have his children,
because - frankly - he was fed up with 'em!

Here's the good news, Lucy . . .
It's been said that what he lacks in size,
he makes up for in quickness.
Here's the bad news, Lucy . . .
It was his last wife who said it!


They don't issue him with a new wedding
licence any more . . .
they just punch the old one.


He's been married so many times,
he has a Direct Debit account at Caxton Hall.


He's the only guy I know who <u>leases</u> his
wedding rings from Garrards!


The last time, he married for better and
for worse . . .
but not for long!


His Wedding Certificate reads;
'To whom it may concern'.


Once bitten, twice broke.


I know he seems to get married a lot but it's
not as if he's so crazy about women . . .
it's <u>wedding cake</u> he's nuts about!


It's better to have love and lust
than never to have love at all.

# THE BRIDE

The days of blushing, virginal brides have all but disappeared. No longer are women considered to be mere appendages to their menfolk. They run businesses, they negotiate, they travel. Very often they are better paid than their husbands.

The bride's speech, once a rarity, may now be here to stay.

Or not.

Either way, here are some suitable lines ...

> I'm a bit nervous today. You see, making a speech is very much like having a baby; it's fun to conceive, but hell to deliver!

> He tricked me into marrying him ... he told me I was pregnant!

> In my experience, there are three types of men; the intelligent, the sensitive and the majority.

> The trouble with a husband who works like a horse is that all he wants to do in the evenings is hit the hay.

> We have a very enlightened vicar. Did you hear him this morning? "Do you take this man for better, or probably worse?".

> Husbands are all very much alike; they just have different faces so you can tell them apart.

Some husbands come in handy around the
house. Others come in unexpectedly!

It wasn't exactly a proposal as such. He took
me out to a Chinese restaurant for a romantic
meal and asked; "How would you like your
rice, fried or steamed?" . . .
I looked him in the eye and whispered;
"Thrown"!

My policy is to let him think he's going to be
bossing the house . . .
when actually, he's going to be housing the
boss!

Husbands are like old kerosene lamps . . .
They're not particularly bright . . .
They often get turned down . . .
They smoke all day . . .
And they go out at night.

Choosing a husband is exactly like choosing a
house . . .
you ignore the way it is and picture how it's
going to be once you've got it remodelled.
                                        (Bridging Line)

Give a man a free hand and he'll run it all
over you.                               *(Mae West)*

Guns don't kill people . . .
husbands who come home too early kill
people!

If all his previous girlfriends were laid end to
end, I wouldn't be at all surprised.

# APPENDAGES

Selected extras which may be appropriate.

## THE SINCERITY SECTION

Oh God! I've been dreading this!

Here are some words to counterbalance the roast lines and cynical gags. Included are some 'positive' one-liners; humorous words of flattery useful for guys and gals who just can't take the other stuff. Some of the guests may actually enjoy listening to this tosh and, in any case, if your speech is packed only with zingers, it'll be all 'ping' and no 'pong'. So let's get it over with, shall we?

> To the bride and bridegroom
> we pledge fifty years of happiness.
> Invite us back for your Golden Wedding and
> we'll be delighted to renew that pledge.

> Lucy ...
> please remember that Dave is yours on approval.
> You may return him for credit or exchange,
> but your love will not be refunded.

> A marriage may be made in Heaven,
> but the maintenance work has to be carried
> out here on earth.

Love grouts wrinkles.

They say that behind every successful man is
an astonished mother-in-law . . .
When Dave's success comes . . . and it will . . .
nobody is going to be surprised,
least of <u>all</u> his mother-in-law.

                              (Bridging Line)

She's a very well-educated girl. Speaks several
languages. Not only can this young lady read
the bottom line of any eye-testing chart,
she can pronounce it!

He's all-man . . . he knows no fear!
He came into the world as a creature of
adventure . . .
the first thing he did when he was born was to
bungee jump with his umbilical cord.

Everybody loves her . . . she's a real charmer.
She has such a wonderful personality that
when she takes a taxi, the driver gives <u>her</u> a tip.

When it comes to food and drink, he's a real
connoisseur. He can tell from one sip of wine,
not only the year it was made . . .
not only the vineyard . . .
but he can tell you the bust measurement of
the bird who jumped on the bloody grapes!

**Merely to call him a computer engineer
is like calling Michaelangelo a <u>decorator</u>.**

See also 'Love and Marriage Quotations'.

*(Hey Madame Editor, do I have to keep writing this
stuff?)*

*Yes* (Ed.)

## *ILLNESS AND BEREAVEMENT*

There's always a danger, when handling certain sensitive
issues such as serious illness or recent bereavement, that
your audience will become sombre and that your speech
will end on a sad and awkward note.

The loss of a dear one has to be acknowledged by at least
one of the speakers, and he risks 'losing' his audience
during what would otherwise have been a sparkling,
laugh-a-minute speech. It's almost enough to make you
wish they hadn't passed away, isn't it?

I always place these subjects about three quarters of the
way through the speech, giving the speech-maker plenty
of time to ease out of the poignant atmosphere and back,
gently, into the laughter.

Of course, the language you use is crucial. Avoid words
like "dead", "killed", "injured", "terminal", etc. and
subsitute gentler language. Try to portray the departed
with a semblance of continuity; here's an example:

> You know, it takes an occasion like this, when
> our close family and our good friends are with
> us, to remind us once again of those who can't
> be with us ... among them, our dear Grandma
> who passed away last year, and who really
> would have enjoyed seeing Dave getting
> hitched ...
>
> And we all remember Dave's late partner and
> best friend Sean, who we lost in August and is
> sadly missed.
> Sean would have been best man today and I'm
> proud to step in for him ...
> in a way, I feel we're sharing the job.
> In any case, Dave was <u>my</u> best man two years
> ago so at last I can get my own back!

However tragic the circumstances of Sean's death, you'll
notice that, while not in any way trivialising his passing,
the words are totally natural and he is treated in a
straightforward manner ... almost as if he were on
holiday.

This way, we've shown respect and affection to our absent
friends, we've kept the audience from sinking into
depression and we're ready to go straight into another
series of one-liners before closing the speech.

Here's another example of how bereavement may be
handled, including a mention of Aunt Fiona's surviving
husband ... In a way, I'm saying; "Max made the effort
and pulled himself together especially for today.". The
lines, you'll notice, get lighter gradually so that you don't
have an unseemly leap from sadness to hilarity.

It really is nice to see so many of both families here today, but we all miss one very special lady, Aunt Fiona ... she would have been very proud to be at Dave's wedding and we all think of her with love on this special occasion. However, we're delighted to welcome Uncle Max, who came along even though he knew full well that I'd be making a speech today. What a sport!

Tonight, the happy couple leave for their honeymoon in Cyprus. As many of you know, when Lucy goes abroad, she likes to learn about local dialects and customs ... I hear that last time Lucy was in Cyprus, she picked up a little Greek ... I hope she doesn't run into him; it might be quite embarrassing.

and so on ...

Treat all illnesses as transient. This doesn't mean you should belittle other people's health problems, but bear in mind that each sufferer handles his or her condition differently.

Be safe. Acknowledge it, but don't dwell on it ... This sort of thing should be fine:

We're all very happy to see Brenda here this afternoon, looking so well after her recent operation.

(Expect applause.)

Brenda, we're really delighted you were able to make it today and that you're obviously well on the road to recovery.

## *IN A MARQUEE*
### *(It happens you know)*

Ladies and gentlemen,
first of all, I must say what a thrill it is to be
making a speech in a room that was once
Pavarotti's night-gown!

Welcome to the marquee . . .
de Sade!

The last time I made a speech in a marquee,
I was so funny I brought the tent down.

My uncle used to be in the tent business,
but it folded.

Ladies and gentlemen,
welcome to Colonel Ghaddafi's time-share!

## *TOASTS*

A toast is a brilliant device; it flatters an ego, it closes a
speech and it gives you an excuse to have a drink.

Here's to the lasses we've loved, lad
Here's to the lips we've pressed
For kisses and lasses, like liquor in glasses
The last is always the best!

(Don't be surprised if the audience shouts: "Boom Boom!".)

Here's champagne to our real friends
And real pain to our sham friends.

Here's to happy days . . .
any twit can have a good time at night.


May you live as long as you want to
And want to as long as you live!


Here's to my mother-in-law's daughter,
And here's to her father-in-law's son,
And here's to the vows we've just taken,
And the life we've just begun.


Here's to the prettiest, here's to the wittiest,
Here's to the truest of all who are true.
Here's to the neatest one, here's to the sweetest one,
Here's to them all in one . . . here's to you.


Grow old along with me,
The best is yet to be,
I've got a credit card,
Between us we've got three.
          *(With apologies to Herbert V. Prochnow)*


Family and friends, here's looking at you . . .
which is why I need this drink!


Here's to our wives and sweethearts.
May our sweethearts become our wives,
And our wives ever remain our sweethearts.

(Puke! Puke!)

To long life and happiness . . .
Your long life will be our happiness.

Here's to love . . .
the only fire for which there's no insurance.

To love . . .
the only game where one pair beats three of a
kind.

Finally, this is what I call a 'groast' . . .
it's a cross between Grace and a Toast . . .

Lord . . . Bless this bunch
While they munch lunch.

## HECKLING

Night club comics often have to cope with loud-mouth
drunks and various nasty customers. The comedian is
usually well-armed with several lines designed to turn the
tables on the smart-ass and to get an extra laugh or two at
the heckler's expense.

At a wedding, however, any heckling is usually very good-
natured and restrained. It would be rather heavy-handed,
if not churlish, for a wedding speaker to learn professional
anti-heckler lines simply for the purpose of silencing
someone enjoying the party.
So here they are . . .

Feel free to speak your mind . . .
I have a spare three seconds.

You know you really shouldn't drink
on an empty head!

Nice suit . . .
were you there for the fitting?

Hey, I always wondered what became of that
kid who played the banjo in 'Deliverance'.

Look at him
The Ghost of Christmas Stupid!

Did you ever get the feeling that
Snow White and Dopey had a baby?

I couldn't agree with you more . . .
In fact, I couldn't agree with you at all!

Hi there! And you certainly are!

Nice to see your voice is working.
Shame it's not connected to anything.

Isn't she a treasure?
I wonder who dug her up.

Hey! I thought alcoholics were meant
to be anonymous!

Is there a new life-form out there that we
don't yet know about?

Oh well, every village has one.

## LOVE AND MARRIAGE QUOTATIONS

A mixed bag of quotes – some original, some borrowed – ranging from the sickeningly sincere to the seriously cynical.

Final score: Cynical: 20  Sincere: 10

**Marriage is a novel where the hero dies in the first chapter.**

**A man is incomplete until he's married.**
**Then he's really finished.**

**Love works miracles every day; it weakens the strong and strengthens the weak . . . it makes fools of the wise and wises up the fools . . . it heightens passion, destroys reason and turns everything topsy turvy.**
 *(Adapted from a quote by Marguerite de Valois)*

**Marriage halves our griefs, doubles our joys and quadruples our expenses.**

**Marriage is an armed alliance against the outside world.**          *(G.K. Chesterton)*

**The best and most beautiful things in the world cannot be seen or even touched. They must be felt with the heart.**          *(Helen Keller)*

Marriage is the process where love ripens into vengeance.

One flesh. *(John Milton)*

Marriage is like a dull meal with the dessert at the beginning. *(Pierre La Mure)*

Many a man in love with a dimple makes the mistake of marrying the whole girl.

The first union to defy management. *(Will Rogers)*

If you have half-a-mind to get married; do it! ... That's all it takes!

An institution that turns a night owl into a homing pigeon. *(Glenn Shelton)*

A wedding is very much like a funeral, except you smell your own flowers.

A man should not insult his wife publicly, at parties. He should insult her in the privacy of the home. *(James Thurber)*

Marriage is an institution.
Marriage is love.
Love is blind.
Therefore, marriage is an institution for the blind.


The sort of woman who could make a fool out
of a man could also make a man out of a fool.


Love is like quicksilver in the hand.
Leave the fingers open and it stays.
Clutch it, and it darts away.
                              *(Dorothy Parker)*


Love is like a curry . . .
you really have to have confidence in it to
enjoy it.


The only life sentence that gets quashed by
<u>bad</u> behaviour.


The surest way to save a marriage from
divorce is not to show up for the wedding.


When it comes to relationships,
Love is the quest . . .
Seduction, the conquest . . .
Marriage, the inquest.


A deal in which a man gives away half his
groceries in order to get the other half cooked.
                              *(John Gwynne)*

Marriage is very much like a pair of shears;
joined together so that they can't be separated,
often moving in opposite directions yet always
punishing anyone who comes between them.

*(Some old twit)*


Many marriages follow a set pattern; first
comes the engagement ring, then comes the
wedding ring ... then comes the suffering.


Marriages are made in heaven -
Divorces are handled by a lower court.


Marriage is like a violin; when the beautiful
music is over, the strings are still attached.


Marriage, after all, is not a lottery ...
you've got a chance in a lottery!


Marriage is nature's way of keeping people
from fighting with strangers.


Most girls seem to marry men who happen to
be like their fathers. Maybe that's why so
many mothers cry at weddings.

# CLOSING MESSAGE

Well . . . this is where I end the book because I'm sick of it now. There's just no way I can win. If your speech is a brilliant success, you certainly won't tell people you got it all from a book, will you? Naah . . . you'll take all the credit yourself, won't you? If it doesn't work, you'll probably write me a letter of complaint and embarrass me in front of my publishers.

Good luck with it anyway.

Now leave me alone.

*(Mitch Murray, 1994)*